Desktop

SHUFFLEBOARD

Slide it!

T0364031

Running Press
Hachette Book Group
1290 Avenue of the Americas, New York, NY 10104
www.runningpress.com
@Running_Press

First Edition: October 2018

Published by Running Press, an imprint of Perseus Books, LLC,
a subsidiary of Hachette Book Group, Inc. The Running Press name
and logo is a trademark of the Hachette Book Group.

The publisher is not responsible for websites (or their content)
that are not owned by the publisher.

ISBN: 978-0-7624-6406-7

CONTENTS

SHUFFLE IT UP!

It is mid-afternoon, and you're falling asleep at your desk. Luckily, you don't have to be an octogenarian on a cruise or a hipster in a pub to enjoy a few exciting rounds of shuffleboard with a coworker. Forget about dealing with full-length courts or cumbersome equipment, because all you need is the *Desktop Shuffleboard* mini table and minimal hand-eye coordination.

YE OLDE SHOVE HA'PENNY

These days you're more likely to associate shuffleboard with cruise ships, or maybe a Brooklyn dive bar, but the game originated in fifteenth-century England, where drunken gentlemen were literally "shoving pennies" across surfaces to pass the time. The game of shove ha'penny (short for "shove half-penny") transcended the boundaries of class in England—you were just as likely to play it in a country estate as a common soldiers' barracks—and was even played by

King Henry VIII. Eventually, the game crossed the Atlantic to arrive in the New World, where it was played in countless bars and taverns across the colonies.

Towards the end of the nineteenth century, the rules and style of the game had changed from the British shove ha'penny into the more familiar shuffleboard, and results could be found in the papers right beside baseball scores and dramatic boxing write-ups. In the twentieth century, table shuffleboard rose and fell in popularity, but now it seems it's here to stay. And while table shuffleboard, bocce, air hockey, and curling might share a similar ancestor, rules, and skillset, sometimes there's nothing better than a group of friends playing a good old game of shove ha'penny.

SET-UP

Now that you're educated in all things shuffleboard, it's time to unpack your *Desktop Shuffleboard* components.

You should have:

- 1 mini shuffleboard table
- 2 mini table inserts
- 4 table stickers
- 3 blue weights
- 3 red weights

Unfold the table and pull each side so you can extend your mini table to its full length. Slide the two extra table pieces into the gap to fully assemble the playing surface. The line (seam) in the middle of the table is the foul line. Remove the 4 stickers, from their backing and attach to the four squares that make up the shuffleboard table—you can check the image to make sure they are in the right place. When you're done, there should be three zones on each side of the foul line. Now you're all set up and ready to play!

HOW TO PLAY

The rules of *Desktop Shuffleboard* are the same as regular table shuffleboard rules. You can play either singles or on a team and a coin toss decides who goes first. If you win the coin toss, going second might actually be your best bet, because the **hammer**, or the last shot taken in a round, is considered to be the most advantageous. If you pick the hammer, then your opponent(s) get to pick the color they want. Once that is all decided it's time to slide!

The goal of the game is to push the weight as far as you can without having it slide off the board; brute force won't get you far, but a timid game isn't going to net you many points either. There are three zones that will allow you to gain points and the foul zone, which is the area between the foul (middle) line and the Zone 1 lines. The higher the zone you land in, the more points you score.

ONE ON ONE

Flip a coin to decide who goes first and assign who plays which color (3 weights per player). Then play begins at one end of the table and each player alternates "shuffling" one weight at a time to the other end, which is now the scoring end.

Players now must score as many points as possible. You may also try to bump or knock off your opponent's weights or even bump your own weights into a higher scoring zone. Once all 6 weights have been shuffled, that concludes the end of the **round**. Now you can tally up the points or collect the weights and go a few more rounds.

TEAMS

In team games, flip a coin to decide which team is going first and assign colors (3 weights per player). Teammates stand at opposite ends of the table and play alternating rounds. Each round is played the same as in one-one-one play, but you'll want to keep track of the score at the end of each round. Once all teammates have completed a round, combine the scores and see which team scored the highest number of points.

SCORING

You can play as many rounds as you want or have time for, but a standard rule is to see which side gets to 15 or 21 points first. If you're really procrastinating, you can play to 51 points. Once you or your opponent reach your predetermined set of points (or it's just time to get back to work) then that player has won the **frame**. If you win "best out of three" frames, then you would say you won the **match**.

ZONES & POINTS

There are four zones on a table shuffleboard and the number of points you win is determined by the zone your weight lands in. Remember from before? The higher the zone you land in, the more points you score. Here is a breakdown of the zones and their points:

- Foul Zone = Zero points
- Zone 1 = One point
- Zone 2 = Two points
- Zone 3 = Three points

Now give your weight a careful shove. It must definitively cross a zone line to earn those points. If your weight lands on top of a line, you receive the lower set of points available. Easy, right?

But wait, there's a catch—you only pick up points if your weights are in front of the other team's weights.

For example, you are playing blue and end up with two weights in Zone 3 and one weight in Zone 1 by the end of the round. Your opponent has two red weights in Zone 2, with a third that never made it out of the foul zone. In this case, you would score 6 points, because only the two blue weights in Zone 3 count are in front of your opponent's weights. Your opponent would not earn any points.

SPECIAL POINTS

HANGERS

If you've got a real slick hand and can shoot a weight to hang just off the side of the board in Zone 3, you'll net four points. But this a risky tactic—if you overshoot and slide your piece

off the board, you're getting no points at all!

KNOCK OFFS

In full-size table shuffleboard, strategically knocking your opponent's weights off the board is an aggressive way of making sure they don't score. In the miniature world of *Desktop Shuffleboard*, this kind of accuracy is much harder and we reward you accordingly. If you manage to knock an enemy puck off the board with your own, that gets you one extra point on top of wherever you land!

There are many variations on the rules for table shuffleboard that we did not include here for simplicity's sake, so once you get the hang of the game feel free to shuffle up the rules and play your way!

WANT TO PUT THE HAMMER DOWN? TRIVIA TIME!

Need a tie breaker or to get back to work? Test your shuffleboard knowledge with this lightning round quiz to determine the champion!

QUESTION #1

Why did Henry VIII allegedly outlaw shuffleboard?

A. He thought it was a waste of money.
B. He thought only noblemen should play it.
C. His wives liked it too much.
D. He thought it distracted soldiers from training.

Answer: D. He thought it distracted soldiers from training.

QUESTION #2

What famous play mentions the sport?

A. The Merchant of Venice

B. The Crucible

C. Who's Afraid of Virginia Woolf?

D. Death of a Salesman

Answer: B. The Crucible

QUESTION #3

In what year was "The State v. John Bishop" court case, which determined shuffleboard to be a game of skill rather than chance (and therefore legal for bars to host)?

A. 1812
B. 1929
C. 1848
D. 1912

SLIDE TO VICTORY!

Whether you want to challenge everyone in the office or at your next dinner party to be the Champion of Shuffleboard, or take what you've earned to the bar (or even a cruise ship with cues!), you've got out some sweet new moves and some serious coordination. Relax, reset, and plot your next match!

This book has been bound using handcraft methods and Smyth-sewn to ensure durability.

Written by Ruoxi Chen.

Illustrated by Mario Zucca.

Designed by Joshua McDonnell.